A Treasury of

Old Testament Heroes

The Stories of Noah, Joseph, Joshua, Samson, David, Daniel, and Jonah

This book is for

August 4, 2007

___Julia___

From

___Pop Pop & Mom Mom___

xo xo

Happy 4th Birthday!

A Treasury of

OLD TESTAMENT HEROES

The Stories of Noah, Joseph, Joshua, Samson, David, Daniel, and Jonah

ideals children's books™

Nashville, Tennessee

ISBN 0-8249-4258-2

Published by Ideals Children's Books
An imprint of Ideals Publications
A division of Guideposts
535 Metroplex Drive, Suite 250
Nashville, Tennessee 37211
www.idealsbooks.com

Printed and bound in Italy

Color separations by Precision Color Graphics, Franklin, Wisconsin

Designed by Jenny Eber Hancock

Special thanks to Robert Perkins of Anderson Merchandisers for
his consultation on this project.

10 9 8 7 6 5 4 3 2

Contents

The Story of Noah

Written by Patricia A. Pingry

Illustrated by Stacy Venturi-Pickett

A long time ago

God said to Noah,

"You must build a

very big

boat."

So Noah built

a **big** boat

just as God said.

The boat was

called the

ark.

Noah's friends

laughed at him.

"That Noah is crazy," they said.

"It never rains
in this desert."

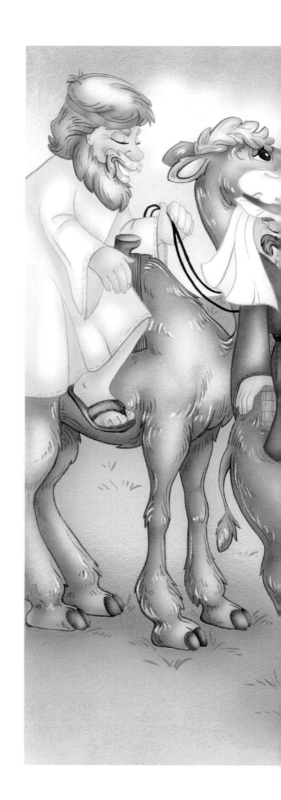

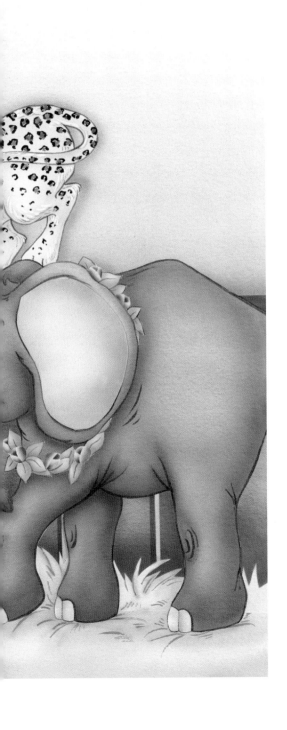

One day,

two

leopards came

to the ark. Then

two

elephants came.

God sent

two

of every

animal

on earth to Noah's ark.

19

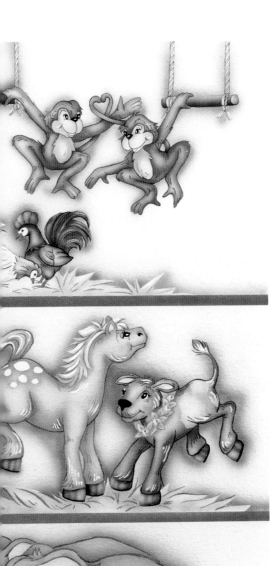

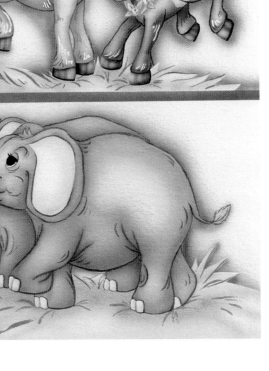

After the

animals

were inside the ark,

Noah went in too.

God

shut the door.

Plop!

went the raindrops.

Crash!

went the lightning.

Boom!

went the thunder.

Noah was not afraid.

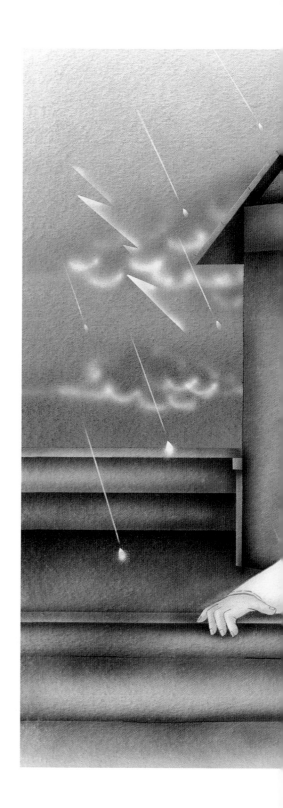

The water rose

higher

and

higher.

The ark began to float.

It rained

forty days

and

forty nights.

Then the rain stopped.

The water went down.

The land was dry.

Noah prayed,

"Thank you,
God,

for a beautiful, clean world."

Noah looked up

and saw colored

stripes in the sky.

This was the very first

rainbow.

"Look

for My rainbow

after every rain,"

God said.

"Then you'll know

I love you."

The Story of Joseph

Written by Patricia A. Pingry

Illustrated by Jim Spence

Jacob had

12 sons,

but he loved his son

Joseph best.

Jacob gave Joseph a

special coat.

His brothers

were jealous

and hated Joseph.

One night, Joseph

dreamed

that his father

and brothers

bowed down to him.

Joseph told his family about his dream. His father was

angry.

His brothers

laughed.

They would never bow down to Joseph!

Joseph's brothers

looked after sheep.

One day, Joseph went

out to the fields

to see his brothers.

They saw him coming.

They jumped on Joseph.

They tore off his coat.

They threw him into a

deep pit.

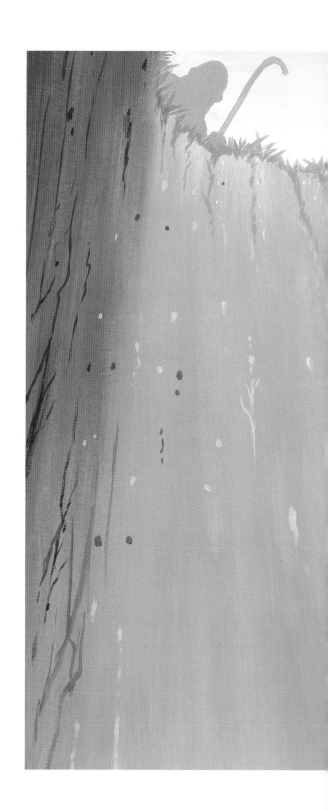

46

Then the brothers

sold Joseph to

some strangers.

They took Joseph

to the land of

Egypt.

The brothers took

Joseph's coat

to their father, Jacob.

He thought

that an animal

had eaten Joseph.

He was very sad.

Later, Joseph became

ruler of Egypt.

One year there was

no rain and no food.

But Joseph had saved

food for Egypt.

Joseph's brothers

came to Egypt for food.

They didn't know that the ruler

was their brother.

Joseph's brothers asked

the ruler for food. They

bowed down

to Joseph.

Joseph said,

"I am your brother.

I love you.

I forgive you

for selling me."

Joseph told his brothers,

"Go home

and bring back

my father."

Jacob was happy

to see his son.

Joseph was a good ruler.

He was a good son.

And he forgave his brothers.

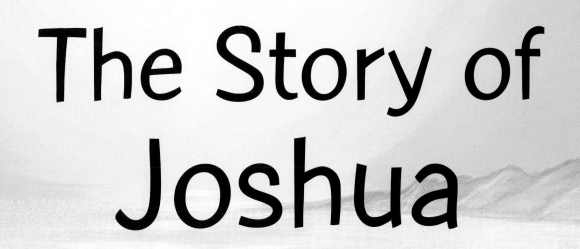

The Story of Joshua

Written by Patricia A. Pingry

Illustrated by Jim Spence

Joshua was leading

his people to

a new home.

One more

river,

one more

town,

then they would be

home.

They all shouted.

The walls of Jericho

fell down!

Joshua and his people prayed,

"Thank you, God,

for taking care of us."

The Story of Samson

Written by Patricia A. Pingry

Illustrated by Stacy Venturi-Pickett

Did you know that

God watches over you?

The Bible tells us that God

watched over Samson

even when Samson

forgot all about God.

90

Samson was a

Nazarite.

He lived for God

and never cut his hair.

Samson was very

strong.

One day he

fought off a

lion

with his bare hands.

The Philistines ruled

Samson's country.

One day, Samson defeated

one thousand Philistines

with just a

bone!

Samson was so strong

that he tore out

the city's gates and

carried them away.

But Samson began to

forget

about God.

Samson fell in love

with a woman

named Delilah.

She asked him why

he was so strong.

She asked

again

and again

and again.

Finally, Samson told her

that he was

strong

because he never

cut his

hair.

When Samson fell asleep,

Delilah called a

Philistine

to shave Samson's head.

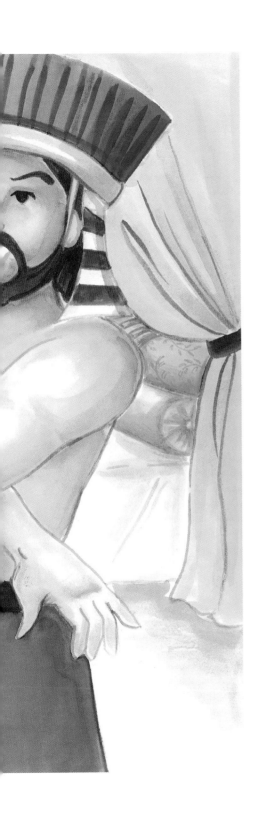

When Samson awoke,

he was no longer strong.

The Philistines put his eyes out.

They took him off to

prison.

But Samson's hair grew back.

One day the guards

took Samson into the temple.

He placed his hands

on the columns

that held up the roof.

108

Samson prayed,

"O Lord, remember me.

Make me strong just

one more time."

Then Samson

**pushed
and pushed.**

The temple fell.

Samson forgot God,

but God still watched

over Samson.

And God will

always

watch over you.

The Story of David

Written by Patricia A. Pingry

Illustrated by

Stephanie McFetridge Britt

David was a

shepherd boy

who loved to

play his harp

for his sheep.

When a lion or a bear

came near the sheep,

David scared it away

with his

slingshot.

One day, David's father asked David to take food to his brothers. They were in the

king's army.

The army was

going out to

fight a giant named

Goliath.

Goliath shook his

fist and yelled at the army.

The soldiers

ran away.

David said,

"Why is God's army scared?"

"Shhh,"

said David's brothers.

"Goliath might hear you."

123

"I will fight the giant,"

said David.

"My Lord has saved me

from lions and bears.

He will save me

from this giant."

The king gave David

armor,

a sword,

and a helmet.

But David

did not want them.

David picked up his

bag of stones

and his slingshot.

He walked out

to meet the giant.

David said to Goliath,

"I come to fight you

in the name of the

Lord Almighty,

the living God."

Goliath laughed.

Goliath rushed

toward David.

David took out

a round, smooth stone.

He placed it

in his slingshot

and slung it

toward Goliath.

The stone

struck Goliath.

"Hooray!
Hooray
for David!"

the soldiers called.

Later, David played songs

about how God

kept David safe,

even when he

faced Goliath.

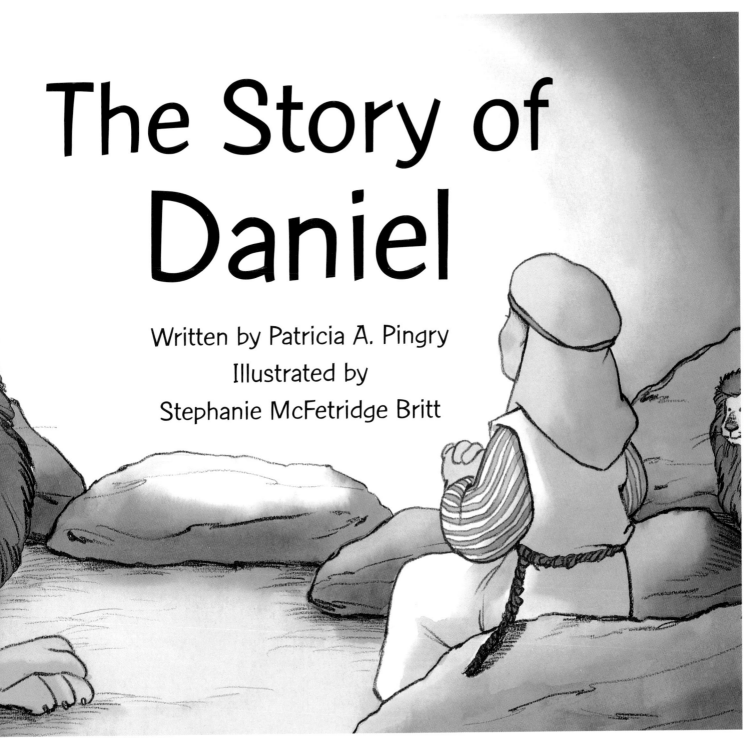

The Story of Daniel

Written by Patricia A. Pingry

Illustrated by

Stephanie McFetridge Britt

There was once a

boy named

Daniel.

Daniel prayed to God

in the morning,

at noon, and at night.

One day the king said,

"Do not pray to God.

Pray to me or you will be

thrown into the lions' den."

But Daniel

would not

pray to the king.

Daniel prayed

only to God.

Some men told the

king

that Daniel

still prayed to God.

148

The king was sad.

He liked Daniel.

But the king had Daniel

thrown into the

lions' den.

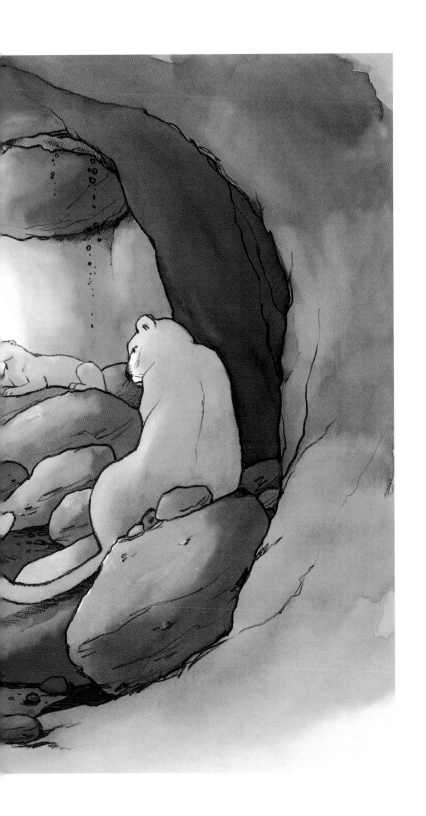

A stone

was rolled

over the opening.

It was dark

in the lions' den.

Daniel prayed

to God.

He asked God

to protect him.

God heard

Daniel's prayer.

God made the lions

stop growling.

The next morning,

the king ran

to the lion's den.

He called out,

"Daniel, did your

God save you?"

And Daniel answered,

"Yes, King.

My God shut the

mouths of the lions."

The king's men

helped Daniel

out of the pit.

Everybody cheered.

162

Daniel went home.

He thanked God

for keeping

him safe.

The Story of Jonah

Written by Patricia A. Pingry

Illustrated by

Stacy Venturi-Pickett

A long time ago

God said to Jonah,

"Go help My people in

Nineveh."

Jonah didn't want

to obey God.

He ran to a boat

going far away.

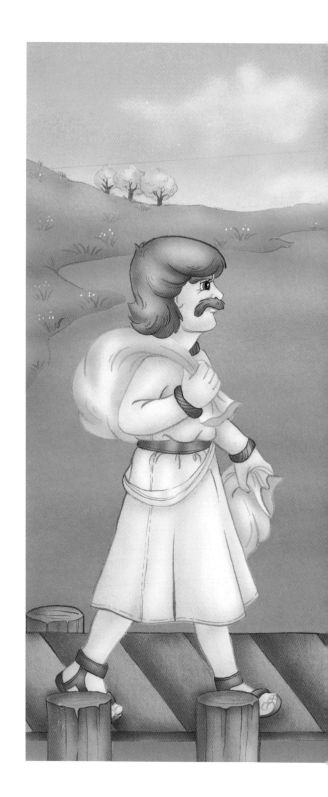

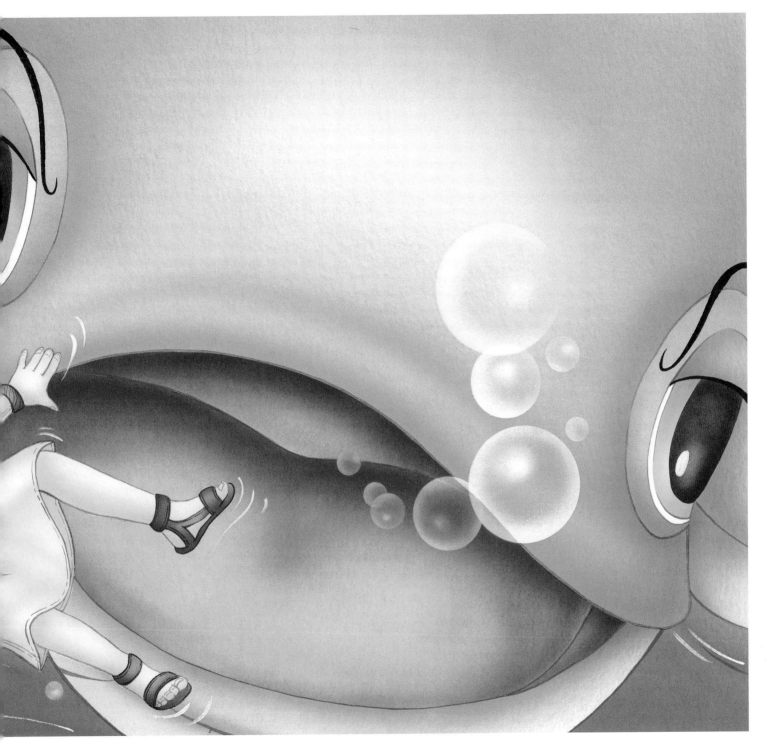

Inside the fish,

Jonah told God,

"I will obey You."

Then the big fish

threw Jonah

out on land.

Then Jonah

obeyed God

and went to help

the people of Nineveh.

189

To Parents:

The stories in this book are simplified versions of the ancient stories that can be found in the Old Testament. Each story provides an introduction to these heroes of old through simple words and colorful pictures. Each story is only about 200 words, so they provide the perfect bedtime story. Parents may also use the stories as a way to introduce, to the very young child, the concept of God's faithfulness.

If you would you like to read the complete Old Testament stories for yourself, you'll find listed on the next page the Bible texts that provided the basis for the stories included in this volume.

Petronella

by JAY WILLIAMS

with pictures by FRISO HENSTRA

Parents' Magazine Press / New York

Other books by Jay Williams

The Cookie Tree
The King with Six Friends
The Practical Princess
A Present from a Bird
School for Sillies
Seven at One Blow
The Silver Whistle
Stupid Marco
The Youngest Captain

Text copyright © 1973 by Jay Williams
Illustrations copyright © 1973 by Friso Henstra

Library of Congress Cataloging in Publication Data

Williams, Jay, 1914-
  Petronella.
  SUMMARY: Determined not to be outdone by her brothers
in seeking a fortune in the world, a young princess sets
out to find a prince to rescue.
  [1. Fairy tales]   I. Henstra, Friso, illus.
II. Title.
PZ8.W6696Pe   398.2′1 [E]   72-6066
ISBN 0-8193-0636-3   ISBN 0-8193-0637-1 (lib. ed.)

In the kingdom of Skyclear Mountain, three princes were always born to the king and queen. The oldest prince was always called Michael, the middle prince was always called George, and the youngest was always called Peter. When they were grown, they always went out to seek their fortunes. What happened to the oldest prince and the middle prince no one ever knew. But the youngest prince always rescued a princess, brought her home, and in time ruled over the kingdom. That was the way it had always been. And so far as anyone knew, that was the way it would always be.

Until now.

Now was the time of King Peter the twenty-sixth and Queen Blossom. An oldest prince was born, and a middle prince. But the youngest prince turned out to be a girl.

"Well," said the king gloomily, "we can't call her Peter. We'll have to call her Petronella. And what's to be done about it, I'm sure I don't know."

There was nothing to be done. The years passed, and the time came for the princes to go out and seek their fortunes. Michael and George said good-bye to the king and queen and mounted their horses. Then out came Petronella. She was dressed in traveling clothes, with her bag packed and a sword by her side.

"If you think," she said, "that I'm going to sit at home, you are mistaken. I'm going to seek my fortune, too."

"Impossible!" said the king.

"What will people say?" cried the queen.

"Look," said Prince Michael, "be reasonable, Pet. Stay home. Sooner or later a prince will turn up here."

Petronella smiled. She was a tall, handsome girl with flaming red hair, and when she smiled in that particular way it meant she was trying to keep her temper.

"I'm going with you," she said. "I'll find a prince if I have to rescue one from something myself. And that's that."

The grooms brought out her horse, she said good-bye to her parents, and away she went behind her two brothers.

They traveled into the flatlands below Skyclear Mountain. After many days, they entered a great dark forest. They came to a place where the road divided into three, and there at the fork sat a little, wrinkled old man covered with dust and spiderwebs.

Prince Michael said haughtily, "Where do these roads go, old man?"

"The road on the right goes to the city of Gratz," the man replied. "The road in the center goes to the castle of Blitz. The road on the left goes to the house of Albion the enchanter. And that's one."

"What do you mean by 'And that's one'?" asked Prince George.

"I mean," said the old man, "that I am forced to sit on this spot without stirring, and that I must answer one question from each person who passes by. And that's two."

"Suppose I wanted to rescue that prince from the enchanter. How would I go about it? I haven't any experience in such things, you see."

The old man chewed a piece of his beard. "I do not know everything," he said, after a moment. "I know that there are three magical secrets which, if you can get them from him, will help you."

"How can I get them?" asked Petronella.

"Offer to work for him. He will set you three tasks, and if you can do them you may demand a reward for each. You must ask him for a comb for your hair, a mirror to look into, and a ring for your finger."

"And then?"

"I do not know. I only know that when you rescue the prince, you can use these things to escape from the enchanter."

"It doesn't sound easy," sighed Petronella.

"Nothing we really want is easy," said the old man. "Look at me—I have wanted my freedom, and I've had to wait sixty-two years for it."

Petronella said good-bye to him. She mounted her horse and galloped along the third road.

It ended at a low, rambling house with a red roof. It was a comfortable-looking house, surrounded by gardens and stables and trees heavy with fruit.

"Good luck," said Prince George. "For I am going to the city of Gratz. I have a feeling my fortune is there."

They embraced her and rode away.

Petronella looked thoughtfully at the old man, who was combing spiderwebs and dust out of his beard. "May I ask you something else?" she said.

"Of course. Anything."

"Where can I find a prince?" Petronella said promptly.

"There is one in the house of Albion the enchanter," the old man answered.

"Ah," said Petronella, "then that is where I am going."

"In that case I will leave you," said her oldest brother. "For I am going to the castle of Blitz to see if I can find my fortune there."

Petronella's kind heart was touched. "Is there anything I can do to help you?" she asked.

The old man sprang to his feet. The dust fell from him in clouds.

"You have already done so," he said. "For that question is the one which releases me. I have sat here for sixty-two years waiting for someone to ask me that." He snapped his fingers with joy. "In return, I will tell you anything you wish to know."

On the lawn, in an armchair, sat a handsome young man with his eyes closed and his face turned to the sky.

Petronella tied her horse to the gate and walked across the lawn.

"Is this the house of Albion the enchanter?" she said.

The young man blinked up at her in surprise.

"I think so," he said. "Yes, I'm sure it is."

"And who are you?"

The young men yawned and stretched. "I am Prince Ferdinand of Firebright," he replied. "Would you mind step-

ping aside? I'm trying to get a suntan and you're standing in the way."

Petronella snorted. "You don't sound like much of a prince," she said.

"That's funny," said the young man, closing his eyes. "That's what my father always says."

At that moment the door of the house opened. Out came a man dressed all in black and silver. He was tall and thin, and as sinister as a cloud full of thunder. His face was stern, but full of wisdom. Petronella knew at once that he must be the enchanter.

He bowed to her politely. "What can I do for you?"

"I wish to work for you," said Petronella boldly.

Albion nodded. "I cannot refuse you," he said. "But I warn you, it will be dangerous. Tonight I will give you a task. If you do it, I will reward you. If you fail, you must die."

Petronella glanced at the prince and sighed. "If I must, I must," she said. "Very well."

That evening they all had dinner together in the enchanter's cozy kitchen. Then Albion took Petronella out to a stone building and unbolted its door. Inside were seven huge black dogs.

"You must watch my hounds all night," said he.

Petronella went in, and Albion closed and locked the door.

At once the hounds began to snarl and bark. They showed their teeth at her. But Petronella was a real princess. She plucked up her courage. Instead of backing away, she went toward the dogs. She began to speak to them in a quiet voice. They stopped snarling and sniffed at her. She patted their heads.

"I see what it is," she said. "You are lonely here. I will keep you company."

And so all night long, she sat on the floor and talked to the hounds and stroked them. They lay close to her, panting.

In the morning Albion came and let her out. "Ah," said he, "I see that you are brave. If you had run from the dogs, they would have torn you to pieces. Now you may ask for what you want."

"I want a comb for my hair," said Petronella.

The enchanter gave her a comb carved from a piece of black wood.

Prince Ferdinand was sunning himself and working at a crossword puzzle. Petronella said to him in a low voice, "I am doing this for you."

"That's nice," said the prince. "What's 'selfish' in nine letters?"

"You are," snapped Petronella. She went to the enchanter. "I will work for you once more," she said.

That night Albion led her to a stable. Inside were seven huge horses.

"Tonight," he said, "you must watch my steeds."

He went out and locked the door. At once the horses began to rear and neigh. They pawed at her with their iron hoofs.

But Petronella was a real princess. She looked closely at them and saw that their coats were rough and their manes and tails full of burrs.

"I see what it is," she said. "You are hungry and dirty."

She brought them as much hay as they could eat, and began to brush them. All night long she fed them and groomed them, and they stood quietly in their stalls.

In the morning Albion let her out. "You are as kind as you are brave," said he. "If you had run from them, they would have trampled you under their hoofs. What will you have as a reward?"

"I want a mirror to look into," said Petronella.

The enchanter gave her a mirror made of gray silver.

She looked across the lawn at Prince Ferdinand. He was doing setting-up exercises. He was certainly handsome. She said to the enchanter, "I will work for you once more."

That night Albion led her to a loft above the stables. There, on perches, were seven great hawks.

"Tonight," said he, "you must watch my falcons."

As soon as Petronella was locked in, the hawks began to beat their wings and scream at her.

Petronella laughed. "That is not how birds sing," she said. "Listen."

She began to sing in a sweet voice. The hawks fell silent. All night long she sang to them, and they sat like feathered statues on their perches, listening.

In the morning Albion said, "You are as talented as you are kind and brave. If you had run from them, they would have pecked and clawed you without mercy. What do you want now?"

"I want a ring for my finger," said Petronella.

The enchanter gave her a ring made from a single diamond.

All that day and all that night Petronella slept, for she was very tired. But early the next morning, she crept into Prince Ferdinand's room. He was sound asleep, wearing purple pajamas.

"Wake up," whispered Petronella. "I am going to rescue you."

Ferdinand awoke and stared sleepily at her. "What time is it?"

"Never mind that," said Petronella. "Come on!"

"But I'm sleepy," Ferdinand objected. "And it's so pleasant here."

Petronella shook her head. "You're not much of a prince," she said grimly. "But you're the best I can do."

She grabbed him by the wrist and dragged him out of bed. She hauled him down the stairs. His horse and hers were in a separate stable, and she saddled them quickly. She gave the prince a shove, and he mounted. She jumped on her own horse, seized the prince's reins, and away they went like the wind.

They had not gone far when they heard a tremendous thumping. Petronella looked back. A dark cloud rose behind them, and beneath it she saw the enchanter. He was running with great strides, faster than the horses could go.

Petronella desperately pulled out the comb. "The old man said this would help me!" she said. And because she didn't know what else to do with it, she threw the comb on the ground.

At once a forest rose up. The trees were so thick that no one could get between them.

Away went Petronella and the prince. But the enchanter turned himself into an ax and began to chop. Right and left he chopped, flashing, and the trees fell before him.

Soon he was through the wood, and once again Petronella heard his footsteps thumping behind.

She reined in the horses. She took out the mirror and threw it on the ground. At once a wide lake spread out behind them, gray and glittering.

Off they went again. But the enchanter sprang into the water, turning himself into a salmon as he did so. He swam across the lake and leaped out of the water on to the other bank. Petronella heard him coming—*thump! thump!*—behind them again.

This time she threw down the ring. It didn't turn into anything, but lay shining on the ground.

The enchanter came running up. And as he jumped over the ring, it opened wide and then snapped up around him. It held his arms tight to his body, in a magical grip from which he could not escape.

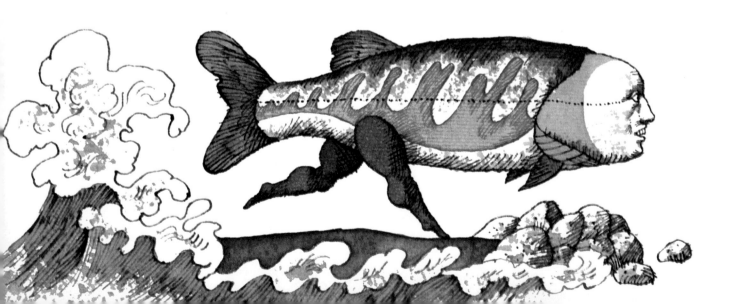

"Well," said Prince Ferdinand, "that's the end of him."

Petronella looked at him in annoyance. Then she looked at the enchanter, held fast in the ring.

"Bother!" she said. "I can't just leave him here. He'll starve to death."

She got off her horse and went up to him. "If I release you," she said, "will you promise to let the prince go free?"

Albion stared at her in astonishment. "Let him go free?" he said. "What are you talking about? I'm glad to get rid of him."

It was Petronella's turn to look surprised. "I don't understand," she said. "Weren't you holding him prisoner?"

"Certainly not," said Albion. "He came to visit me for a weekend. At the end of it, he said, 'It's so pleasant here, do you mind if I stay on for another day or two?' I'm very polite and I said, 'Of course.' He stayed on, and on, and on. I didn't like to be rude to a guest and I couldn't just kick him out. I don't know what I'd have done if you hadn't dragged him away."

"But then—" said Petronella, "but then—why did you come running after him this way?"

"I wasn't chasing him," said the enchanter. "I was chasing *you*. You are just the girl I've been looking for. You are brave and kind and talented, and beautiful as well."

"Oh," said Petronella.

"I see," she said.

"Hmm," said she. "How do I get this ring off you?"

"Give me a kiss."

She did so. The ring vanished from around Albion and reappeared on Petronella's finger.

"I don't know what my parents will say when I come home with you instead of a prince," she said.

"Let's go and find out, shall we?" said the enchanter cheerfully.

He mounted one horse and Petronella the other. And off they trotted, side by side, leaving Prince Ferdinand of Firebright to walk home as best he could.